Did Yo...

DUDLEY

A MISCELLANY

Compiled by Julia Skinner

With particular reference to the work of Dr Paul Collins

THE FRANCIS FRITH COLLECTION

www.francisfrith.com

Based on a book first published in the United Kingdom in 2006 by The Francis Frith Collection®

This edition published exclusively for Bradwell Books in 2012
For trade enquiries see: www.bradwellbooks.com or tel: 0800 834 920
ISBN 978-1-84589-430-6

British Library Cataloguing in Publication Data

Did You Know? Dudley - A Miscellany
Compiled by Julia Skinner
With particular reference to the work of Dr Paul Collins

The Francis Frith Collection
Oakley Business Park,
Wylye Road, Dinton,
Wiltshire SP3 5EU
Tel: +44 (0) 1722 716 376
Email: info@francisfrith.co.uk
www.francisfrith.com

Printed and bound in Malaysia
Contains material sourced from responsibly managed forests

Front Cover: **DUDLEY, MARKET PLACE c1955** D103029p

The colour-tinting is for illustrative purposes only, and is not intended to be historically accurate

CONTENTS

INTRODUCTION

The town of Dudley stands on the ridge of the Pennine Chain; a line running from the top of Cawney Hill, along Hall Street, up the High Street to the parish church, and from there along Stafford Street and the Wolverhampton road lies along the crest of this ridge. To the north of the town is Castle Hill, composed of Wenlock limestone, which has been extensively quarried.

Dudley may not be the largest town, but it is traditionally seen as the capital of the Black Country; the name probably derives from the smoke and dirt of what has for many centuries been an area of heavy industrialisation. The first reference to the name 'Black Country' was in a book that appeared as recently as 1860. The term was used eight years later by Elihu Burritt, then the American consul in Birmingham, when he published a book titled 'The Black Country and its Green Borderland'. Descriptions of the heavily industrialised region in the 17th and 18th centuries often describe scenes of a 'hell on earth', and Elihu Burritt opened his book by describing the area as being 'black by day and red by night'. Thomas Carlyle (1795-1881) wrote of 'a frightful scene (with) a dense cloud of pestilential smoke (where) the whole region burns like a volcano spitting fire from a thousand tubes of brick'.

Exploitation of Dudley's natural resources, with which the area abounded, began well before the Industrial Revolution, including both lime working and mining. The development of industry in Dudley followed the pattern of these natural resources: a 'pool' of coal and associated fireclay and ironstone surrounded the town centre, and the exploitation of these dictated the pattern of settlement and subsequent development of the area. The town centre became the site of many industries, most of which were in the Black Country tradition of 'metal bashing'.

The 20th century saw a steady diminution in the town's traditional industries, notably that of fender and fire-iron manufacture, but at the same time a rise in both light and heavy engineering. This was maintained through to the early 1970s, when the trend was first halted and then reversed following the general economic difficulties of the region and nation.

Perhaps because so many of us can more easily relate to the exhibits in museums such as the superb Black Country Living Museum in Dudley than we can to those in stately homes and mansions, our more recent industrial past has become an attraction in itself that is of great interest. For a long time the name 'Black Country' was almost a term of disparagement, describing a hardworking but unattractive area, but in recent years the growth of the tourist industry has turned the name into a powerful marketing tool that is used with pride.

THE CIVIC GARDENS AND THE CASTLE KEEP c1955 D103039

LOCAL DIALECT WORDS AND PHRASES

'Airn' - hers.

'Appen' - perhaps.

'Bell oil' - effort, as in *'Gi' it some bell oil'*.

'Bin as ow' - because.

'Blartin' - crying.

'Bostin' - very good.

'Franzy' - grumpy.

'Gab' - gossip.

'Jimmuckin' - shaking.

'To kite off' - to run away.

'Mucker' - friend.

'Paces' - sandwiches.

'Puddled' - daft, stupid.

'Reisty' - dirty.

'Spug' - chewing gum.

'Tippon' - Tipton.

'Thiern' - theirs.

'Tranklements' - odds and ends, bits and pieces.

HAUNTED DUDLEY

Dudley is full of ghost stories, and the best way to learn about them is to join one of the Dudley Ghost Walks, which start from the Station Hotel at the foot of Castle Hill. The hotel itself is said to be haunted by the ghost of a former hotel manager, who murdered a servant girl in the cellar when she spurned his advances and threatened to tell his wife. The building was investigated by Derek Acorah of the television programme 'Most Haunted', and he reported that the hotel was actually haunted by the ghosts of two men connected with this story: one is of the murderer himself, and another is of a man who was aware of the crime, and knew where the girl's body was buried. Derek Acorah also felt the presence of the ghosts of two children in the hotel, and another spirit that haunts Room 214, apparently waiting for someone …

Dudley Castle is haunted by several spectres, including a Grey Lady and a Black Monk. Sightings of the monk have been reported by members of staff, and some visitors have experienced feelings of unease which are believed to be due to his presence nearby. The Grey Lady may be the shade of Mrs Dorothy Beaumont, the wife of the Royalist second-in-command who died (possibly in childbirth) during the Parliamentary siege of the castle in 1646, during the Civil War.

A miner who was killed in a rock fall is supposed to haunt the area of Dudley Zoo, and the sound of his ghostly pickaxe can be heard. His ghost was once said to roam near the bear dens of the zoo, and then disappear through a wall.

The Dudley canal tunnel is said to be haunted by the ghost of a man who was murdered there. The ghosts of two children who were drowned after their raft capsized in the tunnel are also supposed to haunt the area.

DUDLEY MISCELLANY

The statue outside the entrance to Dudley's castle, shown in photograph D103004x, opposite, is of William, 2nd Earl of Dudley, and was erected in 1888 'in grateful remembrance of the many benefits conferred by him upon this town'.

Dudley's name is derived from a personal name, Dudda, and the Old English term for a clearing or meadow, 'leah', hence 'Dudda's Leah'. Anglo-Saxon charters of AD779 give details of lands granted to Dudda, a minister of the Mercian King Offa. Other references include one to a Saxon prince called Dudo in AD760, who is said to have 'raised a strong fortress here, which remained until the Conquest', and another, in AD836, to Duda, an ealdorman (a chief or nobleman of the highest rank). Given the date of these references it is unlikely that they all refer to the same person. Over time the name of Dudda's Leah was corrupted and went through several versions: Duddleye (1275), Doddeley (1279), Doddele (1330), and Duddelegh (1360).

Dudley was a manorial borough in the 13th century, sending two members to the parliament of 1295. This status was not uncommon at the time, and may have originated in a charter of 4 November 1218, which conferred rights and privileges upon the 'Burgesses of ye Borrow of Dudley'. Much prosperity flowed as a result of the charter right, which gave exemption from tolls on things bought and sold. This empowered the burgesses of Dudley to hold a market in which they could trade freely without paying the tolls that outsiders were subject to.

FROM THE CASTLE c1955 D103016

Standing as it does on its limestone hill, Dudley Castle dominates the town. It was rebuilt in stone in the early 12th century, but was slighted (damaged to make it of no further military use) in 1175 after its owner, Gervase Pagnell, chose the wrong side in a dispute between Henry II and his eldest son, Prince Henry. The castle passed by marriage to the de Somery family; they rebuilt the fortress in stone, including the keep, gatehouse and curtain wall.

The area around the castle was originally known as the Conigree. In 1817 a circuitous drive was formed around the hill, and walks were laid out traversing the grounds in different directions.

In 1851 a report described Dudley as the unhealthiest town in the country. At that time, one child in every five died here before reaching the age of twelve months.

Almost no building work was carried out at Dudley Castle for the 200 years between 1340 and 1540, but in 1540 John Dudley took over the castle and set about rebuilding the residential block on a grand scale. The results are seen in photograph D103054, below. From the extreme left are a pantry, kitchen, serving place, buttery, hall, and great chamber, most of which had bedrooms above. John Dudley later became the Duke of Northumberland, and tried to set his daughter-in-law, Lady Jane Grey, on the throne of England, after the death of Edward VI. She became known as the Nine Days' Queen, and both Lady Jane and John Dudley were executed by order of Mary Tudor when the coup failed.

THE VIEW FROM THE CASTLE KEEP c1955 D103054

THE CASTLE KEEP c1955 D103019

Some of the last new construction to take place at Dudley Castle
was the windowed building which can be seen in the centre of
this photograph, which was lodgings added c1690.

CASTLE STREET AND ST EDMUND'S CHURCH c1955 D103026

Photograph D103026, above, shows Castle Street before its partial redevelopment in the 1960s, as seen in photograph D103192 on page 16. The church is St Edmund's; a church dedicated to St Edmund has stood on this site since at least the 12th century, and was mentioned in a Papal Bull by Pope Lucius III dated 1182. The original church was demolished in 1646 during the Civil War, and its replacement was not built until 1724. The church was remodelled in the 19th century, and is noted for its unusually long arch.

By the mid 19th century a diverse series of industries had developed in Dudley. One of the most prominent was malting, although this was just about to decline.

The Spout is the local name for the unusually grand fountain which dominates Dudley's lively market place, seen in photograph D103028, below. It was commissioned from James Forsyth by the Earl of Dudley, and was displayed at the Paris Exhibition in 1867 before being installed in its present position. It is an exuberant affair of Italian Renaissance design, with horses, lions and some bizarre but irresistible dolphins. Water flowed from the mouths of the dolphins to fill drinking troughs for cattle and horses, whilst drinking cups, which were filled from the mouths of the lions on each side, catered for human thirst.

THE MARKET PLACE c1955 D103028

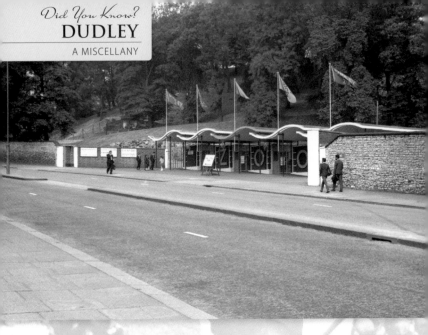

THE ENTRANCE TO DUDLEY ZOO c1965 D103122

The Dudley Zoological Society was founded in 1935 to develop a zoo in the environs of Dudley Castle. The Russian-born architect Berthold Lubetkin was engaged to design the buildings and enclosures. Lubetkin headed the Tecton architectural practice, and as a result the reinforced concrete structures he designed for Dudley have become known as the Tecton Buildings. Photograph D103122, above, shows Lubetkin's stylish entrance turnstiles, which were much admired on the opening day - 6 May 1937 - when 200,000 of the 250,000 people who turned up were refused admission on the grounds of public safety! With over 400 species of animals, Dudley Zoo soon became one of the best in the country, and its advertising slogan became well-known: 'Ooz going to Dudley Zoo?'.

Dudley's growth was fostered by the Dudley Town Act of 1791, under which it was to be governed by Town Commissioners, who held their first meeting on 5 July 1791. They could levy a rate to fund many of the improvements needed at that time, and could also appoint officers to superintend these improvements. The record of the Town Commissioners on health matters was especially poor, and in 1852 the Dudley Board of Health replaced them.

Following the incorporation of the castle in Dudley Zoo, its former entrance was used by the Zoological Society for access to their offices and to the Fellows Club, the white building to the left of photograph D103004, below.

THE CASTLE GATEWAY 1949 D103004

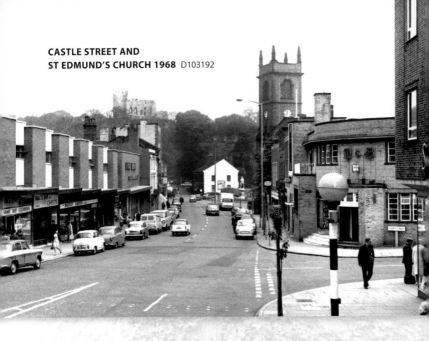

CASTLE STREET AND ST EDMUND'S CHURCH 1968 D103192

Lacking any naturally occurring waterways, Dudley held on to its pre-eminence as a locally important market town of long standing by virtue of its road communications. The 'Pennine Chain crest' route, from Rowley and through the town (Hall Street-High Street-Stafford Street-Wolverhampton Road) was an important packhorse route in medieval times and later. During the 18th century the following roads serving Dudley were turnpiked, whereby each section was established and maintained by a group of investors, with part of the income from the tolls being used to keep the road clear and in good repair: in 1727 Great Bridge, via Dudley Port, through the town centre (Trindle Road-King Street) to Scott's Green (now the A461); also in 1724 Halesowen through Old Hill and Netherton (now the A459); in 1762 Pedmore to Dudley (now the A4036 through Lye); also in 1762 Blackheath via Rowley Regis (now the B4171); and in 1790 Pattingham-Himley and Eve Hill (now the B4176).

During the Civil War, Dudley Castle was the last castle in Staffordshire to be held for the king, surrendering to the Parliamentary forces in May 1646. It was slighted for the second time in its history, and the castle walls, turrets and gatehouse were destroyed, but the residential side was left unharmed.

In 1750 Dudley Castle was reduced to a ruin by a fire; no one was prepared to risk fighting the blaze, which lasted for two days, for fear of the gunpowder which was stored there. The keep, seen in photograph D103007 (below) above one of the later zoo enclosures, is believed to be the oldest substantive part of the castle, with the exception of fragments of walling in the gatehouse, which can be seen to the right.

DUDLEY CASTLE c1950 D103007

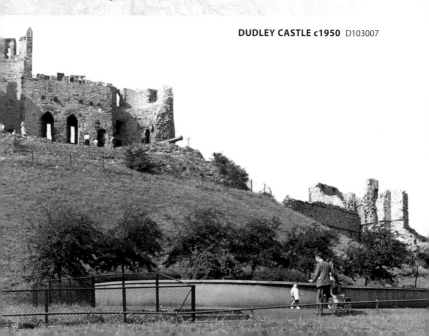

The fountain in the Market Place stands on the site of the Old Town Hall, which was demolished to make way for it. In 1868 it was remarked that the Old Town Hall's 'demolition was generally spoken of regretfully, and the quaint old structure regarded with

MARKET PLACE, LOOKING WEST c1955 D103029

the kindest feelings'. When it was erected c1660 the building boasted many 'modern' facilities, including a whipping post, stocks, and a pillory 'for the correction of malefactors'. In later years it was used as a police station and magistrates' court.

PRIORY PARK c1955 D103043

The Cluniac priory of St James stood about a quarter of a mile west of Dudley Castle. Gervase Pagnell built it in 1161, and the priory prospered until the reign of Henry VIII when it was dissolved. 30 years after its dissolution a visitor observed that it was a great pity 'to see both the church and the monuments defaced as they were'. By 1776 a tanner had set up his business in the ruins, and so had a thread-maker, and by 1801 these had been joined by a glass engraver and a fire-iron polisher. Eventually the Earl of Dudley gave the priory ruins to the people of the town and the council laid out the grounds to form a public park, where people can still sit in contemplation, much as their Cluniac forebears did many centuries earlier.

Persistent local pressure resulted in the passing of a Charter of Incorporation for Dudley on 3 April 1865. Under this instrument the borough was divided into seven wards: St Thomas's, Castle, St Edmund's, St James's, St John's, Netherton, and Woodside. In 1868 the Boundary Act extended the boundaries of the Parliamentary Borough of Dudley to incorporate the Municipal Borough of Dudley, plus the extra-parochial grounds of Dudley Castle Hill and the parishes of Quarry Bank and Brierley Hill and the districts of Pensnett and Brockmoor and of Old Hill and Cradley Heath. In 1888, under the provisions of the Local Government Act, Dudley was declared to be a county borough, and in 1928 a local Act of Parliament enlarged the borough to include the Castle and Castle and Priory wards, formerly in Staffordshire. The West Midlands Order of 1965 further increased the County Borough of Dudley to include Brierley Hill, Coseley and Sedgley UDCs, with effect from 1 April 1966; and the Local Government Act of 1973 created the present Dudley Metropolitan Borough Council with the addition of the former boroughs of Halesowen and Stourbridge on 1 April 1974.

The official name of Dudley's parish church is the Church of St Thomas the Apostle and St Luke, but everyone in Dudley knows it as 'top church' (see photograph D103050a, opposite). This reflects its prominent position on the crown of a hill and at the junction of Upper High Street and High Street. It was erected in 1817 to designs by William Brookes of London, and the Bath stone building cost £24,000, a staggering amount at that time. The tip of the spire reaches 175ft above the ground. Top church has been restored on a number of occasions. During the most recent of these it was discovered that the building has an iron frame - this is most unusual for churches, but not too surprising for an area surrounded by iron works. The dedication of the church is to St Thomas the Apostle, but the parish of St Luke was absorbed into the parish of St Thomas in the 1970s, when St Luke's Church was declared redundant.

Dudley was served by five steam tramway lines, the first of which was in operation from May 1883. The routes were: to Wolverhampton (which ran from 1883 to 1899); to Ocker Hill via Tipton (from 1884 to 1904); to Stourbridge (from 1884 to 1899); to Birmingham via Oldbury and Smethwick (from 1885 to 1904); and to Birmingham via Great Bridge and West Bromwich (from 1885 to 1902). It was also served by seven electric tramway lines between 1899 and 1939: to Stourbridge (from 1899 to 1930); to Cradley Heath (from 1900 to 1929); to Kingswinford (from 1900 to 1925); to Wolverhampton (from 1920 to 1926); to Ocker Hill via Tipton (rom 1907 to 1930); to Birmingham via Oldbury and Smethwick (from 1904 to 1939); and to Birmingham via Great Bridge and West Bromwich (from 1902 to 1939).

THE PARISH CHURCH c1955 D103050a

After the turnpiking of the 18th century, Dudley's basic road network remained unchanged until the building of the Birmingham New Road. This was proposed as early as 1908, but was not fully surveyed until 1922. Construction began in 1924 and was facilitated by government funding to provide unemployment relief. The Prince of Wales officially opened the 9¾-mile road on 2 November 1927. Further road improvements were made piecemeal until the 1960s, when the town centre redevelopment of 1962-69 embraced the widening of King Street and the creation of the Flood Street car parks. Still greater change came with the construction of the Dudley Southern By-Pass in the late 1990s.

The Dudley Zoo buildings were designed by Berthold Lubetkin, who also worked on buildings for London Zoo, and Nikolaus Pevsner waxed lyrical about the quality of Dudley's animal accommodation in his volume on Staffordshire, published in 1974. However, it is hard to be impressed by the sterility of the brutal-looking enclosure shown in photograph D103147, opposite, which in the mid 1960s housed a gorilla, a highly intelligent animal whose native habitat is densely vegetated. Lubetkin's buildings also proved to be difficult and expensive to maintain, but nonetheless the 13 remaining Lubetkin-designed structures on the zoo site now enjoy listed building status. Thankfully, public pressure about zoo conditions since the 1960s has resulted in changed attitudes; much more effort is made nationally to provide an acceptable environment for animals in captivity, and Dudley Zoo is now recognised for the importance of the work done there with its education and animal conservation programmes.

THE ZOO, THE GORILLA c1965 D103147

The regeneration of the south side of Dudley town centre
began in 1962. First to be completed was a pedestrian way
linking Castle Street with the bus station. This was called
Birdcage Walk, and once included an aviary housing tropical
birds. It features a sculptured frieze by the artist Bainbridge

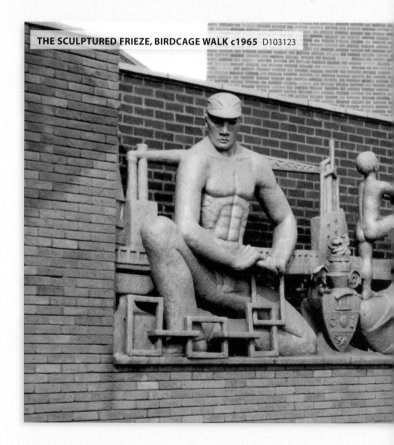

THE SCULPTURED FRIEZE, BIRDCAGE WALK c1965 D103123

Copnall, which was made from fibreglass and powdered aluminium, shown in photograph D103123, below. It measures 25ft by 7ft and depicts, at each end, chain-making and coal-mining, with a mother and child in the centre, representing education.

HIGH STREET AND THE PARISH CHURCH c1955 D103036

It has been estimated that in the early 1600s there were already around 20,000 smiths working within a 10-mile radius of Dudley. They all used wood to fire their forges, and in fact nearly 20,000 trees were needed each year to provide the charcoal for smelting ore in the Black Country before Abraham Darby invented a process in 1709 for smelting iron using coke rather than charcoal, thus saving the country's valuable resources of wood for other purposes. Darby, who is famous for his links with Coalbrookdale in Shropshire, was actually born near Dudley; his pioneering work was one of the triggers of the Industrial Revolution.

Important Dudley industries in the past included nail-making and dealing, cooperage and bag- and twine-making. The manufacture of fire-irons and hearth furniture, little brushes and shovels for making up and tending coal fires, was something of a Dudley speciality, and had evolved out of bedstead and fender manufacture, most of which was concentrated around Wellington Road. The 20th century saw many of these industries contract in scale or disappear from the town altogether, although the fender, fire-iron and bedstead trade survived the longest.

Dudley was served by one trolleybus route, operated by Wolverhampton Corporation, which opened on 8 July 1927. Its terminus was in Stone Street, just off Priory Road, on a cobbled area also used as the site of the town's fish market and public weighbridge. Here the trolleybuses made a very tortuous circle, turning sharply in front of the Saracen's Head to enter the terminus in Stone Street. This became Wolverhampton's last trolleybus route, and was closed on 5 March 1967.

A number of specialist engineering firms became established in Dudley in the 20th century, including those making cars and motor components. These firms were able to capitalise upon land reclaimed from former extractive industries and upon productive capacity built to meet the armament needs of the First World War.

The topography of Dudley town centre precluded its penetration by much of the Black Country canal network. A portion of the Birmingham Canal clips its corner. This canal was authorised on 24 February 1768 and came into use in May 1770. The Dudley and the Stourbridge canal schemes, south of the town centre, were proposed c1774, and were linked by the Dudley tunnel under the town, which opened after seven years of work in 1792. Because of the millions of tons of coal that were being transported on the canals it was deemed necessary to build a second canal, the Netherton tunnel, which runs parallel to the Dudley tunnel and was opened to traffic in 1858. Commercial traffic ceased using the Dudley tunnel in 1951, but it stayed open for recreational use until 1982, when it closed owing to the poor condition of its brickwork. After lengthy repairs the tunnel reopened on 21 June 1992, and was officially opened on 3 September 1992. Visitors to the Black Country Living Museum can take now take a pleasure trip on a narrow boat where they can have a go at 'legging it' through the Dudley tunnel. Lord Dudley & Ward's branch canal was begun c1775 to link the Birmingham line at Tipton with Lord Dudley's lime workings at Castle Mill, where a basin was completed c1779; this now forms part of the Black Country Living Museum site. A later earl also built the Pensnett Canal in the late 1830s. This had no locks and ran for 1¼ miles from a basin at The Wallows to join the Dudley Canal near Dudley Tunnel. It opened in 1840.

A STATUE IN THE CIVIC GARDENS
c1955 D103039X

THE VIEW FROM THE CASTLE KEEP c1955 D103059x

Photograph D103059x, above, shows the view from the castle keep, looking due south across the bus station in Porter's Field. Trindle Road runs across the centre of the photograph, whilst the corner of Hall Street can be seen centre right. A mixture of Midland Red and Birmingham Corporation buses circle the bus station, whilst the National Projectile Factory dominates the skyline. This massive works was erected in 1915, during the First World War, for the production of artillery shells in the build-up to the big push on the Somme in 1916. After the war it was sold to the Co-operative Wholesale Society, who used it to manufacture hollow-ware, mainly buckets, which led to its local nickname of 'the bucket works'.

In 2002 the area of Gornal on the outskirts of Dudley was the epicentre of an earthquake, the largest tremor felt in the UK in 10 years.

The Stourbridge and Dudley Canals were cut in the 1770s and 1780s to provide the Stourbridge glass works with Dudley coal, and for the export of coal and glass to other areas by means of a junction with the Staffordshire & Worcestershire Canal at Stourton. The main line of the Stourbridge Canal swung south and then east around Brierley Hill to meet up with the Dudley Canal at Black Delph Locks, seen in photograph B355004, below.

BRIERLEY HILL, THE CANAL LOCKS c1965 B355004

Motor omnibus services began in Dudley in direct competition to tramways c1924, run by a variety of companies. Formal agreement over the replacement of tramway services on 10 September 1929 saw these operated by the Birmingham & Midland Motor Omnibus Co Ltd, or Midland Red, who came to dominate bus

services in the town. At their peak they operated 47 routes from the bus station in Porter's Field. All Midland Red services were taken over by the West Midlands Transport Services Executive on 1 October 1969, and bus services are now provided by their successor, Travel West Midlands, amongst others.

THE RUINS, PRIORY PARK c1955 D103041

WEDNESBURY, HIGH STREET c1960 W235012

Wednesbury, a few miles north-east of Dudley, was originally called Woden's Bury, and might be the Wodensbeorg mentioned in the 'Anglo-Saxon Chronicle'. If so, then it has a somewhat bloody history. The chronicle records that in AD592 there was a great slaughter in Britain at Wodensbeorg during a pitched battle between the Mercians and the West Saxons, and there was a further battle there in AD715 between the armies of Ine, King of Wessex and Ceolred, King of Mercia.

The Poor Law Amendment Act in 1834 established a system of parish unions for the relief of the poor. Under this, a Dudley Union was formed in 1836, comprising the parishes of Dudley, Sedgley, Tipton, Rowley Regis and Dudley Castle Hill, covering 18,040 acres and 134,125 people. The Union was badly run from the outset, for its Board of Guardians were inefficient. Matters were eventually improved in the 1850s and a new workhouse was built at Shaver's End; this opened in 1859 and later formed the kernel of the former Burton Road Hospital.

THE CASTLE KEEP c1960 D103080

Did You Know?
DUDLEY
A MISCELLANY

Between 1962 and 1969, the south side of Dudley town centre was comprehensively redeveloped under what was called 'the Clearance Area' scheme. This took in most of the old sub-standard buildings and streets south of King Street. The scheme was in three phases, involving the development of Birdcage Walk, with associated shops and car park, the Hall Street

CASTLE HILL, THE JUNCTION WITH TIPTON ROAD c1960 D103076

redevelopment and the Flood Street car park and Churchill Precinct. From the late 1950s onwards, Dudley Council part-funded Dudley Photographic Society to record the Clearance Area ahead of the scheme's commencement. This far-sightedness on their part has left a special record of a now-vanished part of Dudley in Dudley Archives.

Dudley was once well served by railways, having the lines of two different companies meeting at a joint station at the foot of Castle Hill. The first company was the South Staffordshire Railway, which began passenger services from a temporary station at Dudley on 1 May 1850. Passenger services along the 'South Staffs' line continued until 6 July 1964. The second company was the Oxford, Worcester & Wolverhampton Railway (OWW), which began its passenger services from Stourbridge to Dudley on 20 December 1852 and through to Wolverhampton on 1 July 1854. This company was taken over by the Great Western Railway (GWR). Services between Stourbridge and Wolverhampton were withdrawn on 30 July 1962. There was also a line from Old Hill to Dudley, which opened on 1 March 1878, whose passenger services last ran on 15 June 1964. In January 1967 the site of Dudley station was remodelled into a Freightliner Terminal, which opened on 16 July 1967; 20 years and a recession later, falling freight business could not justify keeping this open, and it closed on 28 September 1986.

To mark the millennium a statue of a bronze horse by Andrew Logan was commissioned by Dudley Council, which sits on the Scotts Green Island (roundabout). The horse represents Pegasus, a flying horse from Greek mythology, and is designed to symbolise hope for the future in the new millennium. The wings of the horse are inlaid with glass, a reference to Dudley's glass industry. Andrew Logan said of his work: 'For me, Pegasus is to do with the elements, earth and sky. It's about where we come from and where we are going to'.

SPORTING DUDLEY

Without doubt the most extraordinary sportsman ever to come from Dudley was the England footballer Duncan Edwards. Edwards was a precocious young talent, and became the youngest player to play in Division One when he made his Manchester United debut. He followed this by becoming England's youngest ever debutant. Within a few years he had played 18 times for his country, and had won two League Championships with United. He tragically died as a result of his injuries after the Munich air crash in February 1958. Many commentators have suggested that, had he survived, he would have gone on to be one of the world's greatest players. In 1999 a statue commemorating Duncan Edwards was unveiled in Dudley's town centre.

The largest crowd ever to attend a Dudley Town FC match was 16,500. This was the official attendance at the match to celebrate the opening of the sports centre ground in 1936.

Dudley cricket ground at Tipton Road hosted first-class cricket for over 60 years, from 1911 to 1971. Worcestershire played at least one county championship match at the ground each year. The final game was against Yorkshire in July 1971. Two players scored over 300 not out at the ground, FR Foster of Warwickshire, and EH Hendren of Middlesex.

Dudley's best-known sports personality of recent times is Sam Allardyce. He was born in Dudley in 1954, and began his playing career at Bolton Wanderers. He was a member of the team that won Division Two in 1978, and had a long career, starting at Bolton in 1971, and ending at Preston in 1993. After finishing his playing career he achieved even greater prominence as a manager. He was appointed manager of Bolton in 1999, and over the next few years he established them as a successful Premier League club.

QUIZ QUESTIONS

Answers on page 48.

1. What do the two figures on the top of the fountain in the Market Place represent?

2. Who was Dud Dudley, and what were his two contributions to history?

3. What is the tragic connection between the Dudley area and the Gunpowder Plot to blow up the Houses of Parliament and James I in 1605, which is remembered on 5 November each year?

4. Which famous 'giant greenhouse' was built with materials from Dudley and Tipton?

5. This was made by N Hingley & Sons Ltd of Netherton in 1911; it weighed 16 tons, and at that time it was the biggest example of its kind in the world. A team of twenty horses hauled it to Dudley Station on the first stage of its voyage to the bottom of the North Atlantic - what was it?

6. What is the creature depicted in the sculpture at the Flood Street Island (roundabout) on the Dudley Southern Bypass, and what is its link with Dudley?

7. What would you use a 'tommy hammer' to make?

8. Which comic personality, born in Dudley in 1958, is officially recognised as one of Britain's funniest men?

9. One of the attractions at Dudley Zoo is the Lemur Wood, home to four species of lemurs - ring tailed, black and white, black and collared. Dudley Zoo has one of the largest collections of lemurs in Britain, but from which country do these creatures originate?

10. What is the Dudley Bug, and where can you see one?

THE CASTLE c1950 D103007x

RECIPE

BLACK COUNTRY BEEF STEW

Ingredients

450g/1lb stewing steak
300ml/½ pint mild ale
300ml/½ pint beef stock
225g/8oz black pudding, sliced
110g/4oz mushrooms
2 large onions
½ teaspoonful chopped sage
1 tablespoonful tomato purée
1 teaspoonful chopped parsley
½ teaspoonful chopped thyme
1 bay leaf
Salt and pepper
Oil for frying

Slice the onions and dice the steak. Heat a little oil in a medium sized saucepan and fry the onions until softened. Add the diced steak a few pieces at a time and lightly brown. Add the ale, tomato purée, bayleaf and the finely chopped fresh herbs, and season to taste. Simmer gently for 20 minutes to reduce slightly, then add the stock and simmer for 1½ hours.

Fry the slices of black pudding and mushrooms, and add to the stew. Return the stew to the boil briefly, then serve with new potatoes and green vegetables.

THE MARKET PLACE c1955 D103027

RECIPE

FAGGOTS WITH ONION GRAVY
*Faggots and peas is one of the traditional meals of the Black Country.
This recipe brings the dish up to date with a special gravy.*

Ingredients
For the faggots:
25g/1oz unsalted butter
1 medium onion, peeled and
finely chopped
175g/6oz minced pigs' liver
2 lamb or pigs' hearts,
trimmed and cut into chunks
450g/1lb belly of pork,
trimmed and rind removed
Half a teaspoonful of ground
mace
4 tablespoonfuls freshly
chopped chives
1 teaspoonful freshly
chopped sage
1 egg, beaten

Salt and freshly ground
pepper
115g/4oz fresh white bread
crumbs
25g/1oz beef dripping or
3 tablespoonfuls olive oil

For the gravy:
4 red onions, peeled and with
each onion cut into 8 wedges
4 sprigs of fresh thyme
1 tablespoonful olive oil
900ml/1½ pints fresh beef
stock
290ml/½ pint red wine
Salt and freshly ground black
pepper

Melt the butter in a small saucepan and add the onions. Cook until soft and transparent, then leave to cool slightly. Place the belly pork onto a chopping board and cut into portions. Place the minced pigs' liver into a large glass bowl and place under the blade of a mincer. Using a fine blade of a mincer, mince the pork belly and lamb or pigs' hearts directly into the bowl with the pigs' liver. (If you do not have a mincer at home ask your butcher to mince all your meat for you.) Add the cooled chopped onions, mace, chives, sage, beaten egg and salt and pepper. Stir in the breadcrumbs. Using your hands, shape the mixture into 12 patties. Place them on a plate and chill in the fridge for about 1 hour.

Pre-heat the oven to 200 degrees C/400 degrees F/Gas Mark 6, then place the onion wedges into a large roasting pan or ovenproof dish. Add the thyme and drizzle over the olive oil. Place in the oven and roast uncovered for 40 minutes until the onions are caramelised.

When the onions are cooked, heat the dripping or olive oil in a large frying pan. Fry the faggots until golden brown on both sides. Place the stock and wine in a small saucepan, bring to the boil and reduce by a third. Remove the roasted onions from the oven and lay the faggots on top. Pour over the gravy liqueur. Reduce the oven temperature to 180 degrees C/350 degrees F/Gas Mark 4 and cook the faggots for 40 minutes.

Place two to three faggots onto a plate. Top with a spoonful of the onions and pour over the gravy. Serve the faggots with mashed potatoes and green vegetables, particularly peas.

QUIZ ANSWERS

1. The two figures standing on the top of the fountain in the Market Place represent 'Industry in General' and 'Industry in Particular'.

2. Dud Dudley (born 1599) was one of eleven illegitimate children of Edward Sutton, 5th Baron Dudley, and his long-term mistress Elizabeth Tomlinson, a daughter of a Dudley collier. In the 1620s he claimed to have developed a process for turning coal into coke for use in iron smelting (well ahead of that developed by Abraham Darby in 1709), but had to abandon its use because of violent protests from local charcoal burners, who felt that it threatened their livelihood. He is also famous for producing a map showing Dudley Castle in which he correctly identified the strata of beds of coal and ironstone in the area, which is believed to be the first geological map ever produced.

3. A number of the conspirators of the Gunpowder Plot, including Robert Catesby, the leader, took refuge at Himley House after the plot was foiled. Two men from Rowley Regis, Thomas Smart and John Holyhead, were charged with sheltering them; they were tried and executed in Wolverhampton in January 1606.

4. All the iron and glass for the construction of the Crystal Palace in London for the Great Exhibition of 1851 was provided by the towns of Dudley and Tipton.

5. The anchor of the ill-fated White Star liner, the 'Titanic'.

6. The sculpture, part of the Millennium Trail of stunning modern sculptures around Dudley, features a salamander in flames. Although there is a lizard species known as the salamander, this salamander represents the mythical beast that was said to live in fires, the hotter the better. A salamander also features on the Dudley coat of arms, and is a reference to the numerous furnaces that used to be found in the area. It was incorporated into the design by Dudley's first mayor, whose name, appropriately, was Frederick Smith.

7. 'Tommy hammers' were used to dress the welds in chain-making.

8. Lenny Henry. In 2003, he was listed in The Observer newspaper as one of the 50 funniest acts in British comedy.

9. Lemurs originate from the island of Madagascar, off the south-east coast of Africa.

10. The limestone rocks beneath Dudley are some of the most fossilised in the world - more than 600 different species have so far been identified, dating from the Silurian period. The trilobite fossil *Calymene blumenbachii* is particularly common in the rock; it was used as a symbol of the local limestone mining industry, and also appeared on the town's coat of arms. Its local nickname is the Dudley Bug (sometimes the Dudley Locust). Examples of the Dudley Bug can be seen in the new geological gallery, Dudley UnEarthed, at the town's museum.

DUDLEY FROM THE AIR 1947 AFR7769

FRANCIS FRITH

PIONEER VICTORIAN PHOTOGRAPHER

Francis Frith, founder of the world-famous photographic archive, was a complex and multi-talented man. A devout Quaker and a highly successful Victorian businessman, he was philosophical by nature and pioneering in outlook. By 1855 he had already established a wholesale grocery business in Liverpool, and sold it for the astonishing sum of £200,000, which is the equivalent today of over £15,000,000. Now in his thirties, and captivated by the new science of photography, Frith set out on a series of pioneering journeys up the Nile and to the Near East.

INTRIGUE AND EXPLORATION

He was the first photographer to venture beyond the sixth cataract of the Nile. Africa was still the mysterious 'Dark Continent', and Stanley and Livingstone's historic meeting was a decade into the future. The conditions for picture taking confound belief. He laboured for hours in his wicker dark-room in the sweltering heat of the desert, while the volatile chemicals fizzed dangerously in their trays. Back in London he exhibited his photographs and was 'rapturously cheered' by members of the Royal Society. His reputation as a photographer was made overnight.

VENTURE OF A LIFE-TIME

By the 1870s the railways had threaded their way across the country, and Bank Holidays and half-day Saturdays had been made obligatory by Act of Parliament. All of a sudden the working man and his family were able to enjoy days out, take holidays, and see a little more of the world.

With typical business acumen, Francis Frith foresaw that these new tourists would enjoy having souvenirs to commemorate their days out. For the next thirty years he travelled the country by train and by pony and trap, producing fine photographs of seaside resorts and beauty spots that were keenly bought by millions of Victorians. These prints were painstakingly pasted into family albums and pored over during the dark nights of winter, rekindling precious memories of summer excursions. Frith's studio was soon supplying retail shops all over the country, and by 1890 F Frith & Co had become the greatest specialist photographic publishing company in the world, with over 2,000 sales outlets, and pioneered the picture postcard.

FRANCIS FRITH'S LEGACY

Francis Frith had died in 1898 at his villa in Cannes, his great project still growing. By 1970 the archive he created contained over a third of a million pictures showing 7,000 British towns and villages.

Frith's legacy to us today is of immense significance and value, for the magnificent archive of evocative photographs he created provides a unique record of change in the cities, towns and villages throughout Britain over a century and more. Frith and his fellow studio photographers revisited locations many times down the years to update their views, compiling for us an enthralling and colourful pageant of British life and character.

We are fortunate that Frith was dedicated to recording the minutiae of everyday life. For it is this sheer wealth of visual data, the painstaking chronicle of changes in dress, transport, street layouts, buildings, housing and landscape that captivates us so much today, offering us a powerful link with the past and with the lives of our ancestors.

Computers have now made it possible for Frith's many thousands of images to be accessed almost instantly. The archive offers every one of us an opportunity to examine the places where we and our families have lived and worked down the years. Its images, depicting our shared past, are now bringing pleasure and enlightenment to millions around the world a century and more after his death.

For further information visit: www.francisfrith.com

INTERIOR DECORATION

Frith's photographs can be seen framed and as giant wall murals in thousands of pubs, restaurants, hotels, banks, retail stores and other public buildings throughout Britain. These provide interesting and attractive décor, generating strong local interest and acting as a powerful reminder of gentler days in our increasingly busy and frenetic world.

FRITH PRODUCTS

All Frith photographs are available as prints and posters in a variety of different sizes and styles. In the UK we also offer a range of other gift and stationery products illustrated with Frith photographs, although many of these are not available for delivery outside the UK – see our web site for more information on the products available for delivery in your country.

THE INTERNET

Over 100,000 photographs of Britain can be viewed and purchased on the Frith web site. The web site also includes memories and reminiscences contributed by our customers, who have personal knowledge of localities and of the people and properties depicted in Frith photographs. If you wish to learn more about a specific town or village you may find these reminiscences fascinating to browse. Why not add your own comments if you think they would be of interest to others? See **www.francisfrith.com**

PLEASE HELP US BRING FRITH'S PHOTOGRAPHS TO LIFE

Our authors do their best to recount the history of the places they write about. They give insights into how particular towns and villages developed, they describe the architecture of streets and buildings, and they discuss the lives of famous people who lived there. But however knowledgeable our authors are, the story they tell is necessarily incomplete.

Frith's photographs are so much more than plain historical documents. They are living proofs of the flow of human life down the generations. They show real people at real moments in history; and each of those people is the son or daughter of someone, the brother or sister, aunt or uncle, grandfather or grandmother of someone else. All of them lived, worked and played in the streets depicted in Frith's photographs.

We would be grateful if you would give us your insights into the places shown in our photographs: the streets and buildings, the shops, businesses and industries. Post your memories of life in those streets on the Frith website: what it was like growing up there, who ran the local shop and what shopping was like years ago; if your workplace is shown tell us about your working day and what the building is used for now. Read other visitors' memories and reconnect with your shared local history and heritage. With your help more and more Frith photographs can be brought to life, and vital memories preserved for posterity, and for the benefit of historians in the future.

Wherever possible, we will try to include some of your comments in future editions of our books. Moreover, if you spot errors in dates, titles or other facts, please let us know, because our archive records are not always completely accurate—they rely on 140 years of human endeavour and hand-compiled records. You can email us using the contact form on the website.

Thank you!

For further information, trade, or author enquiries
please contact us at the address below:

**The Francis Frith Collection, Unit 6, Oakley Business Park,
Wylye Road, Dinton, Wiltshire SP3 5EU.**

Tel: +44 (0)1722 716 376 Fax: +44 (0)1722 716 881
e-mail: sales@francisfrith.co.uk **www.francisfrith.com**